THE USHER'S BOOK

Creating a Welcoming and Safe Environment for Worship

JOHN P. GILBERT

Abingdon Press
Nashville

THE USHER'S BOOK
CREATING A WELCOMING AND SAFE ENVIRONMENT FOR WORSHIP

Copyright© 2005 by Abingdon Press

ISBN 978-0-687-03862-6

07 08 09 10 11 12 13 14—10 9 8 7 6 5 4 3 2
MANUFACTURED IN THE UNITED STATES OF AMERICA

CONTENTS

INTRODUCTION

"You take the lady's left hand in your left hand and place it over your right arm before you escort her to her seat . . . "

No, no, no!

That was church ushering a couple of centuries ago. It had its time and place, but the twenty-first century is as different from that time as our modes of travel—airplanes and automobiles—are from that time of horse-drawn buggies.

Ushers are still absolutely essential in every church. Yes, *every* church, no matter how few are the worshipers in that congregation. Ushers are a critical part of the worship team, that collection of folks who by their special talents, gifts, and abilities are designated to lead the congregation in the worship of God. And ushers are crucial because ushers perform two very important ministries or functions in today's congregations.

Those functions, ministries, are

      1) **Welcoming** and

      2) **Insuring comfort and safety**.

Your job as an usher is to extend a warm and genuine welcome to everyone who comes near the door of the church. And your job as an usher is to be absolutely sure that every person in that church is comfortable, safe, and secure from the time he or she arrives on the church property to the time she or he leaves.

This booklet is going to describe the ministry of ushering in today's church in terms of those two functions. You will grow weary of hearing about welcoming and comfort and safety; but these are the ushers' tasks, and unless the ushers attend to them faithfully, all kinds of problems can arise.

One more important point! Ushers have important ministries to fulfill, but those ministries are best fulfilled unobtrusively. That is, the best usher is the person who does the job without calling any attention to herself or himself or to the job being done.

Oh yes, another quick comment. This little booklet is written for small and medium membership congregations. The megachurches have all kinds of policies and procedures for ushers; these are excellent, but seldom meet the needs of the congregation that has one hundred fifty or fewer worshipers each week. So this booklet is designed for the vast majority of congregations who number worshipers each Sunday in two or low-three digits.

So welcome to the ministry of ushering in the place where the people of God gather to worship and be the community of faith.

1

WHAT—AND WHO—MAKES A GREAT USHER?

W hat are ushers about? Right! Providing a welcome for those who come to worship and insuring the comfort and safety of those who worship. So who makes a good usher? Let's mention a few points right at the outset.

- **Ushers can be and are both women and men.** Nothing anywhere at any time has ever said that ushers had to be all of the same gender.

- **Ushers are called to this ministry by God.** Serving as an usher is just that—*service.* And who is being served? By serving the people of God, the community of the church, the usher is serving God. Are you getting a point here? Ushers have to be committed Christians! They have to be folks who know and love the Lord, who are dedicated to the church, and who are willing to give of themselves in service.

- **And—here's one that may cause some trouble—ushers should be older teens or adults.** Yes, it's cute to have children dressed in their Sunday best serving as ushers, handing out worship bulletins, and the like. But the task of ushers is the task of *welcoming* and *providing comfort and safety* for worshipers. This demands a level of maturity and skill that children simply do not possess. You'll learn more about this as we focus on the safety dimension of what ushers do.

- **Ushers must be "people people."** That is, they must genuinely like people of all kinds. They must be at ease with people, both those whom they know and those they have never seen before. They must be genuine and sincere. They must be attentive to their tasks and reflect both the joy and the seriousness of the congregation at worship.

- **In short, and of utmost importance, the ushers should be the first persons a worshiper encounters at the church.** This means that the ushers go a long way toward setting the tone for the day and dictating the kind of worship experience the worshiper may have. Just imagine yourself entering a church in which you've never worshiped before. No one speaks to you. No one greets or welcomes you. No one hands you a worship bulletin or even indicates which of several doors lead to the nave.[1] You stumble around unsure of yourself and finally sit down in a pew. Or you approach the narthex[2] of a church in which you've never worshiped before. The door is already open; and a smiling person is just inside the door, not blocking your way, but standing just to the side as you enter. This person greets you warmly with a genuine smile, thanks you for coming, hands you a worship bulletin, shows you to the nave, and suggests where you might sit. Which of these two experiences is more likely to put you in the proper frame of mind for worship?

So where do you find these ideal persons to serve your church as ushers? They are folks who are already right there in your congregation. They are young and they are old. They are men and they are women. They are wealthy and they are financially strapped. They are long-time members of the congregation and they are newcomers. They are persons of various races and nationalities and even languages. Sometimes, they are the folks who have not often been asked to serve on committees or task forces. Sometimes they are not what the rest of us call "able-bodied." One of the most effective ushers I ever met used a wheelchair, but her joy and enthusiasm for the people of God and for the gospel of Christ made her stand ten feet tall!

How do you enlist and organize ushers?

This is an area that some of the older books on ushering spent countless pages discussing. But that misses the point, I believe.

Ushers can be enlisted by the worship committee, by the lay leader, by the outreach and evangelism work area, by an usher board, or even by the pastor. Some churches ask adult Sunday school classes to provide ushers for each service of worship. Some other churches have elaborate usher training and fancy schedules posted in the narthex. Many churches enlist ushering teams, and these teams take turns serving the church in this way. And still other churches invite couples to serve as ushers on a rotating basis.

I hope you're getting a couple of important points here. One is that no one way to enlist and assign ushers is right (or wrong) for every congregation. Another point is that ushers should be *rotated;* that is, different persons should serve as ushers on different Sundays. The old idea that Joe Smith has served as usher every Sunday for the last sixty-five years has gone by. Rotate ushers. Rotate them weekly or rotate them monthly. But rotate them. Why? You know the answer to that: You are involving more persons in the worship leadership of your congregation! You are allowing more persons in the congregation to answer their calls to service and ministry.

And I hope you caught another important point in the foregoing comments. I've used the word *enlist* several times with reference to securing ushers. And that's exactly what I mean. To enlist someone for something in the service of God and the church means that

- **you talk with that person directly;**
- **you describe the task you have in mind for that person in detail;**
- **you indicate why you think that person "fits" that task and what has led you to believe that God may be calling that person to that task; and**
- **you invite that person to pray about his or her response before giving you an answer.**

Don't ask for volunteers to serve as ushers or say to someone, "We're desperate for ushers; we've asked everyone else, so now we're asking you." Prayerfully identify those folk in your congregation that God may be calling to this special service.

You want to know how many ushers you need to enlist? That's a good question!

Remember we're thinking of small and medium-sized membership churches in this booklet, so let's say this:

I believe you need at least *four* ushers each Sunday for a church of any size. You'll discover why I say this in later chapters of this booklet. You may need more! How do you know? If folk enter your nave by more than one major door, you need additional ushers. If you have a church-in-the round with many aisles in the nave, you may need more than four ushers for the offering and for serving or for guiding folk to the Sacrament of the Lord's Supper. So how do you know how many ushers you need? Try this: Start with four ushers for each Sunday; try this out for about a month, then add more ushers as you sense that you need more.

OK. You've enlisted four teams of four ushers each and you're going to rotate teams weekly, that is, team one takes the first Sunday of the month, team two the second Sunday, and so on.

Name one person on each team to be responsible for that team. Use any title you like—chief or head usher, team captain, coordinator, or whatever. By any title, this person's task is to call each member of her or his team during the week before they are scheduled to serve as ushers. This person will make sure that all the ushers can be present, on time, and ready to serve. If one team member cannot serve on the particular Sunday, the team leader should have a list of backups, probably members of one of the other teams. The team leader needs to contact a backup no later than Friday evening (if possible), inviting that backup person to serve as usher on the coming Sunday. Are you getting the hint here? You do *not* wait until Joe or Susie does not show up on Sunday morning, then grab someone at the last minute and beg them to serve as usher. Of course, there may be a last-minute exception, but in that case as well, ask a person from the backup list.

Now: What, specifically, is it that these ushers do?

2

BEFORE THE SERVICE BEGINS

(What was it we said ushers do? Right! Ushers are responsible for *welcoming* and for *providing comfort and safety* for worshipers.)

Your day as an usher begins long, long before the service of worship commences! In fact, your day of service should begin the moment you awaken and offer a prayer that your service might be acceptable to God and that you might faithfully fulfill the duties and privileges of serving the congregation as an usher.

Your first task as an usher is prayer. Seek God's guidance and presence as you prepare to serve. This prayer will set the tone for your whole day. Please do not neglect it! (Yes, by all means, make this a spoken prayer, and ask your family to join you in this time of prayer.)

The next step in serving as an usher? What are you going to wear to serve God and the congregation by ushering today?

Of course, your church may have very specific policies regarding what ushers are to wear. In some congregations, white dresses or black suits may be not only customary but part of the congregation's policy. If you wish to serve your congregation as an usher, abide by the policies in place.

But what if your congregation has no specific policies about how ushers are to dress? What should you wear?

In some ways suggesting what *not* to wear is easier than telling you what to wear. Put most simply, do not wear anything that calls attention to yourself. Dress respectfully and appropriately. You are serving God, not showing off your latest finery.

But let's get a bit more practical. Take your clues about what dress is appropriate from the congregation. If most of the men in the congregation wear suits and ties, then please do not usher in jeans and a polo shirt. Or if most of the men in the congregation wear khakis and open-neck shirts to church, then you may call undue attention to yourself if you dress in a three-piece suit. Get the point? The same goes for women serving as ushers. If no one wears a feathered hat and white gloves to church on Sunday, then your white gloves and fancy hat are going to be out of place. If most of the women wear dresses to church, then serving as an usher in slacks and a sweatshirt may be inappropriate. Remember: Do not dress in a way that calls attention to yourself; think twice about big dangling earrings or loud comedy neckties or neon-colored sport coats or multiple clanking bracelets and necklaces.

Many congregations ask their users to wear identifying badges of some sort. This may be a colored cloth flap that fits into a pocket, a plastic badge that is pinned or clipped on, or even a white flower to be worn in the lapel. If your congregation expects such identification, do it! (Ladies, if the cloth flap that is designed for a man's suit coat breast pocket doesn't seem to work because you have no pockets, then simply pin it on.)

OK. You've prayed and selected your attire. Now it's time to head to church.

Time to head to church? Yes! But your time as an usher to be at church is at the very least *forty-five minutes before the service of worship begins.* If your Sunday school meets before the worship service, you may have to excuse yourself from your class on the Sundays you usher. You are going to be busy! Here's a quick check-list of some of the things you as an usher need to do before folk arrive for the service of worship. Add your own ideas to the end of this list.

In the sanctuary:
- **Check the thermostat in the sanctuary.** Is it set right? Will folk be comfortable when the sanctuary is full? Yes, this may be the task of some designated others, but a quick check is still in order.
- **Are all the proper lights on?**
- **Glance at the exit signs that are required in your sanctuary.** Are they lighted as they should be? While you're at it, check the fire extinguisher, also required. Has it been serviced on schedule?

The pews:
- **Check the hymnal racks on the backs of the pews.** Are hymnals in each space? Are the hymnals all right side up and facing in the same direction? (Yes, it's a little thing, but it says something about the seriousness of the service of worship.)
- **What about attendance register pads?** Are they where they are supposed to be? With pencils in them?
- **Do a quick check of the pews.** Pick up scraps of paper, gum wrappers, and, if the church had an early service, worship bulletins that have been left in the pews.

On the chancel:
- **Paraments[3] may not be your responsibility, but be sure the right colors are in place and that the paraments are straight and neat.** Know where the paraments calendar is, and check it if you're not sure of the color for the day. (A paraments calendar is a calendar that indicates the appropriate liturgical color for each Sunday and holy day of the year. Your church should have such a calendar near where the paraments are stored.)
- **Check the candles.** Are they of equal height? Are they sufficiently long to burn throughout the service? (If you use the metal tube candles, be sure to check the inserts. These have an annoying way of burning down without anyone noticing.)
- **Is the water in the pastor's tumbler fresh?** Can the pastor reach it easily, if needed? Some pastors like a cough drop or two in a handy place on or inside the pulpit. Other pastors like a handkerchief or facial tissue within reach in or on the pulpit, and still others want a pen or pencil within easy reach.
- **If your choir sits in the chancel, check for hymnals in the choir loft.**
- **If your congregation uses a public address system, be sure the microphones are where they are supposed to be.** You may not be responsible for the operation of the sound system, but hand-held microphones have a habit of "walking away." A quick check will assure you that all are where they should be.

- **Are the offering plates or receptacles where they should be?** If the plates were used at an earlier service today, has the offering been removed and stored safely for counting?

In the narthex:
- **Are the doors unlocked?** You'd be surprised how many folk come into the church through doors other than the main sanctuary doors. But when that first worshiper comes to that main door, she or he expects the door to be open!
- **Check the worship bulletins.** Are they the right bulletins for today's date? Sometimes last week's extra bulletins are left in the narthex, and folk pick them up thinking they are this week's.
- **What about the candlelighters—the metal "sticks" that your acolytes use to light the candles on the Communion table?** Again, this may not be your responsibility, but check to be sure the candlelighters are in their proper place, that they have sufficient tapers (the long waxed strings) in them for this service of worship, and that at least two ways of lighting the candlelighters are at hand. (Asking if someone has a match at the last minute shows a lack of concern!) In some congregations, supervising the acolytes is part of the ushers' responsibilities; in other congregations, specially appointed persons help the acolytes robe (if that is the custom), light the candlelighters, and move into the nave at the proper time.
- **Many churches have a supply of visitor information cards or packets stored in the narthex.** Check this supply to be sure enough are on hand and that the packets are complete. (These packets often include a visitor information card, a brochure about the church and congregation, some information about the denomination, and usually a pen or pencil with the church's name and worship times printed on it.)
- **The narthex should contain some essential supplies at every service of worship.** These supplies include *facial tissue,* a small container of *drinking water* (if no running water is available in the narthex), a *first-aid kit,* and at least *one armchair.* Why these items? Again, *comfort* and *safety.* Of course, (except for the armchair) these items should not be obvious or "on display," but every usher should know where each of these items is.

- **Another hint. Tidy up the narthex; it's the first part of the church building folk see.** Umbrellas, gloves and mittens, and occasionally coats get left there. These can be arranged neatly. If your narthex has a literature table, straighten this also. We are welcoming folk to the house of the Lord; we should care as much about how this house looks for company as we do about our own homes when company comes.
- **And of course, every person who is called to the service of ushering should have at her or his fingertips basic information about the building: Where are the restrooms, drinking fountains, nursery, telephone, wheelchair, and so on.** (Yes, every church ought to have a wheelchair available, both for emergency use during services of worship and to loan to folk in the church or the community who have a short-term need for a wheelchair. This need not be the latest and fanciest chair, but it should be accessible, sturdy, and clean.)

I hope you're getting the essential point here. The ministry of ushering involves providing for the welcome, comfort, and security of all those who come to worship. This cannot be carried out in a haphazard or "last minute" way. You as an usher are a vital and important member of the worship team; in a very real sense, you set much of the tone for each worshiper's experience. Ushering demands your very best; and no detail, no item to check, is too small to be considered. Be early, be ready, and be responsive!

3

WHEN WORSHIPERS BEGIN TO ARRIVE

Are you ready? You've checked and double-checked all the things that need to be right before the service begins. All is in readiness for the worship of God.

Wait! One more thing to do before worshipers begin to arrive. You as a team of ushers should gather in the narthex or some other convenient place for a moment of prayer. Pray that as you respond to God's call to serve the Lord and the congregation as an usher, you may be truly welcoming and that you may be open to God's Spirit among you and the entire congregation. This need not be a long, elaborate prayer; far better are a few words spoken from the heart by one of the ushering team members. In fact, rotating this opportunity and privilege among the members of the team gives each a sense of the presence of God as you serve in God's house as an usher.

Folk will be arriving in just a few moments. What do you do now? Take your stations!

At least one usher should be stationed at each of the doors by which folk enter your worship space. This includes the doors worshipers use as they come from Sunday school or other activities that are taking place. If your church has a narthex (vestibule), then ushers are stationed just inside the narthex.

Each usher should have a stack of worship bulletins in hand, ready to give to those who come to worship. Here's a hint: Hold the bulletins upside down and face (or cover) up in your hand so that you give each person a bulletin right side up and face up as he or she enters.

But before you hand a worshiper a bulletin, greet each worshiper cordially.

What does *cordially* mean? This word can mean many things; some of those meanings are implied in this list of dos and don'ts:

- **Do stand near the door of the narthex, but not *in* the doorway.** A person standing in the middle of a doorway appears to be blocking the door; a person standing just beside the doorway offers a visual welcome and greeting.
- **Smile!** You are welcoming persons to the worship of God, who has given us all things. This is a joyful time; let your demeanor reflect your joy in the Lord and your joy in the presence of this particular worshiper.
- **If you know a person by name, by all means call that person by name—including children!** Treat children who come to worship just as you would treat adults.
- **Greet every person with a welcome *to the worship of God*.** Your welcome is not necessarily to this particular church or this particular congregation, but to the worship of God.
- **If persons come with winter coats or umbrellas, point them to the coatracks or umbrella stands, but do this *after* you have greeted them and welcomed them to the worship of God.** Offer to help them with their heavy outer garments, but do not assume that everyone would want or would welcome such assistance. Take your clues from the worshiper.
- **Hand each person—including each child—a worship bulletin.** (Some churches do not use worship bulletins; if yours does not, a simple word of greeting in the name of the Lord will suffice.)
- **If persons must pass through a second door from the narthex into the sanctuary, open this door for them and hold it open until they are safely inside.** Or, if this door can be kept open (yet out of the way), keep it open.
- **Do *not* engage in small talk with folk as they arrive, such as who won yesterday's game, the latest recipe, or how the fishing has been lately.** But if you know that a worshiper or a member of the worshiper's family has been ill, you may feel free to inquire about the person who is ill.

- **Do *not* reach out to shake hands unless a worshiper *first* extends a hand to you.** Take your clues from the person; recall that some folk suffer from maladies such as arthritis that make their hands sore and tender. A "hearty handshake" from an usher may be a painful experience for some worshipers.

- **Do *not* touch a worshiper on the shoulder, elbow, or back, no matter how good a friend you might be of that person.** This restraint on your part is a demonstration of respect for that person. Recognize that some worshipers may reach out to touch you on the shoulder, back, or arm; accept these as gestures of friendship.

- **Do *not* ask a person or family if she or he or they are visitors or if this is the first time worshiping with the congregation.** Sometimes members who have not attended in some time are put off by ushers who do not recognize them. Of course, if persons indicate that they are visiting, then welcome them cordially and genuinely and offer to be of any assistance. You may be responsible for giving visitors a welcoming packet, or this may take place during the announcement time in the service of worship.

- **Do *not* try to tell persons or families where to sit in the sanctuary unless they ask you to do so or unless they seem bewildered and lost.** If a family indicates that they are visiting or attending for the first time, you might ask them if they prefer to sit near the front or near the back of the sanctuary. But be careful about directing them to a seat in such a way that they feel they must sit where you put them. If they do not indicate a preference, it is perfectly appropriate for you to walk with them and *suggest*, not direct, a place to sit. Where should they sit? If you can place a visiting person, couple, or family near an already seated church family, do so. Introduce the seated church family to the visiting family. Please avoid seating visitors or newcomers in areas where no one else sits; few things make persons seem more unwelcome than to be seated in the center of an island of empty pews. After seating the visitors, return to your station promptly; do not "visit" with others seated in the sanctuary as you make your way to the narthex.

- **And please do not make small talk with the other ushers in the narthex.** Among several things that are especially disturbing to arriving worshipers is a knot of ushers talking and chuckling together and ignoring arriving worshipers or "leaning out of the circle" of ushers to hand persons worship bulletins as they go by.
- **Always, always, always remember that you represent the congregation and by extension the presence of God in this place.** You are the first person the worshiper encounters as she or he arrives at the church. That first impression must be one of genuine and personal welcome and one of both the joy and seriousness of worshiping God together as the community of Christians.

Folk have arrived for the service of worship, the prelude is beginning, and the time of worship has arrived. Here are a couple of last-minute responsibilities for the ushering team just as the service of worship begins.

- **Close (but do not lock) all the outside doors except perhaps the main door into the narthex.** More than one service of worship has been interrupted by a stray dog or other animal wandering in an open door!
- **One usher should do a quick check of the entire building and grounds.** Be sure that everyone is in the sanctuary for worship. What does this mean? Check the kitchen; tell the folk chatting over the last of their Sunday school coffee that worship is beginning. Remind those teens who are in the gymnasium that they are due in worship. Check the youth lounge and invite those who are still there to make their way to worship. Go out to the playground or the church yard and be sure that all the children are inside as they are supposed to be. Yes! This check calls for a great deal of tact, gentle firmness, and love. You are not "shooing" folk into the sanctuary, but you are inviting them to the worship of God. On a practical level, you are insuring the safety of folk—teens left in the gymnasium or youth lounge, children left in the church yard or playground, even adults visiting in the kitchen may, heaven forbid, face many kinds of crises, accidents, or other problems.

- **The usher who is doing this quick tour of the entire building and grounds might check lights and other electrical devices (TVs, VCRs, tape and CD players, space heaters, and so forth), adjust thermostats, insure that the office or study door is closed, that the copier is turned off.**
- **What do we do about telephones?** In this day and age, worshipers should know to turn off their cell telephones as they arrive at church. But the church telephone must be operational, as a worshiper might need to be reached in an emergency. Keeping that telephone operational yet unobtrusive might mean turning the ringer on the telephone to "low" if the ring can be heard in the sanctuary. This would mean, of course, that one usher should be stationed near enough to the telephone to hear it ring even at lowest volume. If no telephone is near the sanctuary, the congregation would do well to make arrangements to station a person in, say, the church office during the worship hour in order to handle any emergency calls. This person could be an usher or someone else designated by the worship team.
- **One more item: The ushering team should gather very quickly and quietly in the narthex to "check signals" as the service is about to begin.** Are any worshipers expecting telephone calls? Have any worshipers expressed any special needs? Has the pastor or the choir director asked for any special assistance during the service? Remember: *Welcoming* and *comfort and safety.* Be sure each of these has received careful attention.

Then the service of worship begins, often with a time of informal announcements.

4

THE SERVICE OF WORSHIP BEGINS

The worship service has begun. Perhaps the pastor is sharing greetings and announcements with the congregation or perhaps the prelude is playing, signaling the time of preparation for the service of worship. You are an usher. What are you supposed to do now?

Stay at your post!

At least one usher should be stationed just outside each door that enters into the sanctuary. This usher's main task is to assist latecomers, to provide a welcome, and to insure comfort and safety. More about that in a moment. But first let's look at two other ushers and their tasks during the service of worship.

The Chancel Usher

One usher, not one stationed by a door, must be seated in the sanctuary, perhaps near the back. This usher has a both simple and difficult responsibility. For the entire service of worship, this usher must have her or his eyes glued on the chancel, and especially on the liturgist and the preacher. This usher's task is to anticipate and to respond to any needs that the liturgist or the preacher may have. Few things break the sense of worship more than the preacher having to ask, "Would someone do this or get that?" The usher stationed in the sanctuary must be alert to whatever needs may arise and must instantly respond to them. What kinds of needs? Listen: Is the liturgist's voice coming across all right, or does the cordless microphone need a new battery? Of course, you as the chancel usher know where those batteries are kept. Is the preacher coughing and clearing her throat a bit? She may need more—or fresh—

water. Get the idea? All kinds of situations arise in the course of a service of worship, and you as the chancel usher are serving the Lord by serving the Lord's spokespersons, the liturgists and preacher, in this case.

Note that the chancel usher must be *seated* in the sanctuary. This means that the chancel usher is a fully worshiping member of the congregation. This usher stands when the congregation stands, sits when the congregation sits, sings the hymns, participates in the recital of the creed, and all other aspects of worship. Remember what we said a couple of chapters ago? An usher never draws attention to herself or himself. And one sure way to do that is to stand in the back of the sanctuary throughout the service of worship like some officer of the law. But, while you as chancel usher are worshiping, you are also keeping an eagle eye on the chancel and all that is taking place there, ready in an instant to provide whatever might be needed.

The Congregation Usher

If your ushering team is sufficiently large (or if you have few doors into the sanctuary so another usher can be seated in the congregation), assign a second usher to sit in the back of the sanctuary as (for lack of a better term) the congregation usher. This usher's responsibility is to focus not on the chancel and what is taking place there, but on the members of the worshiping congregation. Again, this must be done unobtrusively and subtly, but the congregation usher must be aware of what is taking place in and among the congregation at all times during the service of worship. Are many folk fanning themselves or pulling their jackets or sweaters more tightly around themselves? Perhaps the sanctuary thermostat needs adjusting. One congregation usher in a rural church with open windows in the sanctuary heard rain begin to fall outdoors. He quickly scanned the congregation and noticed folk on one side of the sanctuary slide just a bit away from the windows. Silently and unobtrusively he slipped to that side of the sanctuary and closed the windows where the rain was blowing in. That's the kind of thing a congregation usher does.

In another service of worship, the congregation usher noticed that a gentleman was nodding and swaying in a strange manner. The congregation usher slipped into the pew beside the gentleman, put an arm around him, and held him just before he fainted. Fortunately, two other ushers noticed the congregation usher's movement, and one was at the man's side with a wheelchair almost instantly while the other was telephoning for medical assistance. This was a congregation of fewer than one hundred worshipers, yet the ushers handled this situation so well that not all members of the congregation were even aware that something had happened.

One more story: In a small membership congregation, an older lady arose and slowly and painfully began to make her way toward the door leading to the restroom. The congregation usher in this case was a man; he gently tapped the shoulder of a woman sitting near him and asked her to assist the lady. Again, the whole episode caused hardly a stir in the congregation.

Of course these are one-in-a-million stories, but they do happen, just as the story of the congregation usher who noticed (and gently "evicted") a stray dog that had made its way into the sanctuary through the open doors on a warm spring morning is true.

Are you getting the idea here? These two ushers, stationed in the sanctuary, are crucial to insuring the comfort and safety of the congregation and of those leading the congregation in worship. Ninety-nine out of one hundred Sundays they are simply part of the worshiping congregation; but on that Sunday when something special is needed, these ushers are ready and prepared.

The Door Ushers

The ushers seated just outside the doors to the sanctuary have several very important tasks. As with all the tasks related to ushering in the congregation, these are focused on welcoming and on providing comfort and safety.

The first and perhaps most obvious task of the door ushers is to welcome those who arrive late for the service of worship. The welcome extended by the usher to the latecomer must be no less sincere and genuine than that provided for those who arrive on time. Again, it is a welcome to the worship of God as part of the community of believers. Of course, this verbal welcome must often be spoken in quiet tones lest the welcome be heard by those just inside the sanctuary door, but it is a genuine welcome nonetheless. Under no circumstances ever make any kind of comment about the worshiper's tardiness. If the worshiper wants to tell you that he or she had car trouble or some such thing, do not engage in a conversation. Simply say, "We're glad you're here to worship the Lord this morning." An usher and a latecomer in the narthex trying to diagnose a mechanical problem in the latecomer's car is totally inappropriate. (Usher: If you know about cars, fine. But tell the latecomer you'll be happy to help her or him with the problem following the service of worship.)

When do you allow a latecomer to go into the service of worship? When do you open the sanctuary door for the person who arrives after the service has begun? Please work this out with your pastor well in advance. Develop a simple policy with the pastor, and stick with it carefully. For example, most pastors would counsel against persons coming into the sanctuary during the invocation or other prayers, during the Scripture readings, or during a choral anthem or special music. Some pastors permit latecomers to be seated during the announcement time, during the singing of a hymn, or during a spoken call to worship. But please check this out with your pastor well in advance.

If your sanctuary is full, be alert! Tell latecomers where they might be seated with the least amount of disruption to the rest of the congregation. If the latecomers are visitors, your welcome is no less genuine, but you may need to escort them to a vacancy in a pew rather than allowing them as strangers to wander into a sanctuary with which they are not familiar, looking for a place to sit.

Another suggestion: If latecomers arrive with coats, umbrellas, and so on, gently encourage them to remove these and leave them in the narthex rather than struggling out of bulky winter overcoats while seated in a service of worship that has already begun.

That's the welcoming dimension of your responsibility as a door usher.

Your other very major responsibility is insuring comfort and safety. Here are some thoughts.

If an adult comes out your door during the service of worship, quietly, gently, unobtrusively inquire if you can be of any assistance. This does not mean you need to hover or to "dig" for the reasons why the person stepped out of the service. But it does mean making yourself available to help if the person is in need. Here's where that stash of cough drops or facial tissue might come in handy. Here's where your knowledge of the location of rest-rooms, drinking water, and a telephone is crucial. And in some cases, here's where that armchair might be needed. "I was feeling like I needed some air; just let me sit for a moment and I'll be fine." Almost every usher who has served for more than a year has heard this several times.

But—and this is a major *but*—if a child comes out your door, you have a different set of responsibilities; be sure you attend to these responsibilities carefully!

Most children will leave a service of worship in order to go to the restroom. If a child comes out your door and indicates that he or she needs to use the restroom, then you must walk with that child to the restroom, and you must wait outside the door of the restroom until the child comes out. Do not go into the restroom with the child. When the child comes out of the restroom, walk with her or him back to the sanctuary, open the door, and be sure she or he returns to her or his seat. (You are exactly right: If two ushers or adults can walk a child to the restroom door and back again, that is even better than a single usher doing so. But in many small membership congregations this is not feasible.)

OK. What if the child asks for your help in the restroom or if the child lingers in the restroom what seems to be an inordinate amount of time? Then you must enlist the help of an additional usher or adult. If the child is a girl (and you are male), get two women to assist the child or to check on the child. If the child is a boy (and you are female), get two men to assist the child or to check on the child. Never go into the restroom with a child alone.

Why all of this? In this day and age, a congregation cannot be too careful. You must accompany a child to the restroom to insure that that is where the child is going and that the child gets there and returns safely. The swing set right outside the window or the building blocks in a Sunday school room may be too enticing for the child. (Tragically, several cases have occurred of children being snatched while alone in the hallways of a church on a Sunday morning.) What about the two adults in the restroom with a child? This is to eliminate any possibility of accusations of abuse of any kind. (Again tragically, several incidents have taken place that make such safeguards absolutely necessary.)

Suppose the child wants a drink of water. Go with the child to get the drink and stay with the child, returning with her or him to the sanctuary. If your church is equipped with drinking fountains, be sure that the fountains are equipped with sturdy step stools that will allow children to reach the water for themselves. Again, do not pick up a child or hold a child so that she or he can get a drink from a fountain. If no step stool is available, use a paper cup at the drinking fountain for the child.

(Are you getting a not-so-subtle message here? *Hands off children!* Sure, you can shake hands with a youngster, give one a "high five," or even give a special child a bear hug, but not unless the child's parents are present—right there!—and you know from past experience with them that they are amenable to this physical contact with their child.)

What about teenagers who come out of the service? The same procedures hold for teens. But with youth, an additional temptation may be to visit the kitchen or the gymnasium or the youth lounge rather than returning to the sanctuary. Your kind and gentle presence with the teen will encourage him or her to do what needs to be done and to return to the sanctuary as soon as possible.

A hint: Some children or youth may take a bit of offense at your going with them to the area of the restroom or drinking fountain. "I know where it is; you don't need to go with me." Respond with kindness, gentleness, firmness, and a smile. You are not a police officer or a hall monitor; you are a Christian friend ensuring the comfort and safety of that child, that youth (or that adult). That's your calling as a usher in the house of the Lord.

One more quick comment for the door ushers: The temptation is always present to engage in conversation and even perhaps a bit of laughter with folk in the narthex or hallway. Avoid that temptation! You are assisting in the service of worship, not entertaining folk or engaging in a fellowship time. Any conversation must be whispered and brief lest those who are worshiping be disturbed.

To recap: During the service of worship, ushers are part of the worshiping community. Ushers worship as the congregation worships. But ushers have additional duties, be they chancel ushers, congregation ushers, or door ushers. Take these responsibilities seriously! Your ministry is the ministry of *welcoming* and *insuring comfort and safety.*

5

THE OFFERING

Simply sitting by the door and assisting persons who need to leave the service of worship for a variety of reasons is not your only task during the service of worship. In many congregations, you are also responsible for assisting with the *offering*.

Let's get a couple of things straight before we begin, however. Assisting with the offering is not "taking up the money." The offering is an integral part of the service of worship; it is one of the responses to the Word; it is one of the ways the community of faith reacts to the proclamation of the Good News. While we often think of the offering in terms of contributions of money, the offering can take many other forms. Sometimes, the offering will be an offering of time or talent; at other times the offering may be an offering of prayer; at other times the offering may be an offering of presence.

But whatever form an offering takes, it is a response to the Word read and proclaimed; it is the recognition on the part of the people that God alone is the source of all that they have and all that they are; and the offering is giving back to God a portion of what God has given to them for the upbuilding of the kingdom of God on earth. The offering is an act of worship; it is one of the primary ways in which the worshipers participate in the liturgy of the service of worship; that is why it is a crucial component of a service of worship—and, by the way, it is why the modern practice of using credit cards or automatic bank drafts misses the point entirely!

Another word here: Christians are called to tithe, that is, give God the first tenth of all things. But the tithe is not a gift or an offering; according to the Scriptures, the tithe already belongs to God.

Giving a tithe is giving to God what is rightfully God's. Offerings and gifts are what we give to God over and above the tithe; offerings and gifts are what we give because we want to give. That's why many liturgists speak of presenting to God *God's* tithes and *our* offerings and gifts.

Tithing is not a condition of salvation; it is God's grace, not our actions, that saves us. But tithing is the recognition that we are God's and that all that we have is to be used according to God's will. To recognize God's dominion over us is to participate in the tithe.

(If you're beginning to get the idea that those who serve as ushers in the public worship of God ought to tithe as a witness and expression of their own faith, good! That's the point! You do not have to tithe in order to be an usher—no one knows whether you tithe or not; that's between you and God—but your service to God and the congregation through the ministry of ushering will be deeply enriched if you reflect your faith in the tithe.)

Now to the mechanics of ushering during the offering.

First, sit down with your pastor and understand thoroughly how she or he integrates the offering into the service of worship. The way in which this integration takes place will dictate to a degree how the ushers are to handle this dimension of the service of worship. Although the offering takes place in different places within the service of worship, most often the offering takes place following the reading of Scripture and the proclamation of the Gospel—be that in sermon, music, or any other form. Again, this is because the offering is a response to the Word of God.

Who presents this offering to God?

The answer is obvious: The congregation, the worshiping community, presents the offering to God. It is not the minister or the ushers or anyone else who presents this offering to God; it is the worshiping community, the congregation of believers gathered together in the name of Christ. Ideally, then, each member of the congregation could (and in some churches does) come forward to present an offering to God in response to God's Word read and proclaimed. But in most churches, this is not practical, so the ushers, representing the gathered community of Christians, collect the offerings of the people and present them to God for the people.

Is this why the ushers march shoulder to shoulder down the center aisle at the time of the offering? Perhaps, but this is not the most effective way to do this. Because the ushers represent the community, the ushers should come up out of the gathered community. This means that the ushers move from their stations at each door and in the narthex toward the Communion rail or the front of the church in order to receive the offering. This gives the gathered congregation both the visual and the experiential sense that the ushers are truly representing them, that is, coming from all parts of the nave or sanctuary.

Practices differ widely; but in many churches, the ushers gather at the Communion rail or the front of the sanctuary to receive the offering plates from the pastor or liturgist, from an acolyte or the acolytes, or to take the plates from the Communion table.

Offering plates? In most of our churches, metal or wooden plates are used to receive the offering. These plates often have felt or some other sound-absorbing material in the bottom to soften the clink of metal coins. In some churches, baskets or cloth bags with wooden handles are used.

In most cases, the church will provide an offering plate and two ushers for each section of the nave. That is, if a church has a center aisle with two sides or sections of pews, that church will probably have four ushers and two offering plates. Clearly, only two of the four ushers can be handed an offering plate. To continue with this example, most often the two ushers in the center of the four would be handed the offering plates.

Next, in many churches the pastor or liturgist will offer a brief prayer prior to the offering. According to your custom, you may be handed an offering plate before or after this prayer. In either case, however, your demeanor during these moments is crucial. Please: As you approach the Communion rail, walk erect, confidently. (Men: Button that jacket; it just looks better.) Stand tall as you stand at the Communion table, rail, or front of the church, back to the congregation. No hands in pockets! Decide as a team what you will do with your hands. Those ushers who are handed plates will have both hands on opposite edges of the plates, most often holding them level. The ushers who are not handed plates should stand with their arms and hands comfortably at their sides, not clasped behind their backs (in the "Parade Rest" position) or clasped in front of them. We're not describing standing rigidly "at attention" here, but we are describing standing erect, alert, and ready to serve.

Once the prayer is completed, the ushers turn toward the congregation and "pass the plates." This means simply that the usher with the offering plate gives it to the person sitting on the aisle of the first row. That person puts her or his offering in the plate and passes it to the next person in the row. When the plate has moved across the row, the usher at the other end of the row receives it from the person sitting on the aisle and hands it to the person sitting on the aisle in the second row. This continues until the plate has been passed in the last row.

A couple of suggestions: In many of our smaller membership congregations, the numbers of persons sitting in the various sections of the nave are uneven. However, those ushers who are serving a less-full section should slow the process somewhat to stay somewhat even with the team serving the fuller section of the nave. (This is not a race; the pair of ushers who reach the last row first are not the winners!) The process simply looks better if the teams of ushers move through the congregation in an approximately parallel pattern.

Please, usher, do not greet your friend as you are passing the plate to her or him or receiving the plate from him or her. This is not the time for small talk or chit-chat. Stand erect as you are waiting for the plate to make its way across the row to you.

Also, resist the very natural urge to place a hand on the end of the pew back as you wait for the offering plate to move across to you. This simple motion can become a leaning on the pew back by the time you get to the back of the sanctuary. Please just stand erect (though not stiff) at the end of the pew as you wait for the plate.

And in many churches ushers are asked to count the worshipers as they are receiving the offering. If you are asked to do this, learn to do this as unobtrusively as possible. Please do not point your finger or nod you head at each person in the row as you count; even moving your lips as you count can be a distraction. Remember, this is a very serious component of the service of worship. Members of the congregation are worshiping in a vital way as they present their offerings. Anything you do to distract from this sense of worship should be avoided.

In many congregations, the offering plates with the tithes and offerings in them are brought to the Communion table, the chancel rail, or the front of the sanctuary at the conclusion of the offering. This is often accompanied by the singing of the Doxology or some other appropriate hymn. Think of the symbolism contained in this simple act! You as representatives of the congregation are bringing before God the tithes and offerings of the congregation, the congregation's response to God's Word read and proclaimed. Most appropriately, all the offerings are brought to the front of the sanctuary and given to the liturgist or preacher as the Doxology is being sung; in many congregations the preacher or liturgist turns and lifts the offering plates toward the cross as a symbolic gesture of presenting these to God. Ideally, the offering plates with the tithes and offerings in them remain on the Communion table or altar throughout the rest of the service of worship.

(Yes, in some churches the offerings are taken out the back door as soon as they are collected. This may be necessary in some situations, but it denies the congregation an important symbolic act and experience.)

Again, a couple of quick comments about bringing the offering plates forward.

First, you are representing the congregation and presenting their offerings to God. Consequently, please do not amble, stroll, and wander down the aisle with the plates. Move briskly; you are about to represent the congregation before God. If all four ushers (back to our example) bring the offerings forward, walk two by two and try (without a lot of obvious effort) to walk in step or at least remain side by side.

In most cases, the first pair of ushers carry the filled offering plates and the other two ushers move to the outside of these two at the Communion rail or the front of the sanctuary.

If you are carrying the offering plates, glance quickly at the plates before proceeding down the aisle. If a check is unfolded and face up in the plate, quickly and unobtrusively turn it over so that it is face down. Our tithes and offerings are between God and us; they are not intended for everyone—or anyone—to see.

At the conclusion of the Doxology, the liturgist or preacher may have a prayer or dismiss the team of ushers in some other way. When dismissed, turn "smartly" and return to your station.

Turning toward the congregation with a bewildered look on your face destroys the liturgical moment of the offering. In other words, this is not the time to check your count, look for your family members, or speak to a congregant. Simply return to your station.

Special Situations

Yes! Folk in wheelchairs can serve as the ushers who take the offering. This works better if someone pushes the person using a wheelchair. People with other physical disabilities that hinder their mobility can also serve. If so, the other ushers simply adjust the speed of their movement to match that of the person who walks with difficulty.

And another "special situation." What happens if a member of the congregation or the usher drops an offering plate? Yes, it happens, and the clatter can be deafening!

First, if the plate is empty, simply pick it up and proceed. If you retain your composure, the congregation will retain its composure. If you look at the congregation and grin, shrug, or make some gesture, the liturgical moment will be lost.

If the plate is full, pick up the plate, but do not scramble around under the pews trying to pick up the scattered contents of the plate. Simply get the plate (unless it has rolled under the pews into a very awkward position) and proceed. When the service is completed, gather the offering that has been dropped; you will probably find that congregants have gathered the offering and will eagerly return it to you.

Again, the offering is an integral part of the service of worship; it is a high liturgical moment, for it represents the congregation's response to the love and grace of God. An usher will participate in the gathering of the people's tithes and offerings as a humble privilege, honoring both the persons giving their tithes and offerings and our Lord who receives them. Participating as an usher in the high holy time of offering is a sacred moment for all concerned.

6

HOLY COMMUNION

Stop right now!

Don't even read this chapter unless and until you have had an extensive discussion with your pastor, worship committee, or liturgist about Communion. Holy Communion (also called the Lord's Supper, Eucharist, or the Sacred Meal) is one of the highest and holiest elements of any service of worship. Those who have primary responsibility for worship in your congregation—the worship committee, the pastor, the liturgical team—have clear ideas about how the Lord's Supper is to be served. You are part of the worship team, yes; but you are not in charge of the worship team. So your role is to listen, learn, and understand how Holy Communion is served in your congregation, then to serve it in that way. Your role is not to tell the pastor or worship committee how to serve the sacrament; your role is to serve in the time of worship and to carry out any part assigned to you as part of the celebration of the Lord's Supper.

That being said, a few comments about the Sacrament of Holy Communion:

A sacrament is a means and a sign of God's grace. Because a sacrament involves our whole being—sight, sound, touch, taste, and smell—a sacrament puts us closer to God than we are at many other times. Yes, you're right. We are always close to God. What a sacrament does is makes us realize in a total and very intimate way that closeness to God.

A sacrament is something instituted by Jesus Christ and something in which Jesus participated. In most Protestant churches, two sacraments are celebrated: Baptism and Holy Communion. (Our Roman Catholic sisters and brothers observe seven sacraments—Baptism, the Eucharist, confirmation, marriage, orders, penance, and extreme unction. Most Protestants do not observe all of these as sacraments because, for example, we have no evidence that Jesus Christ was confirmed, married, ordained, or received extreme unction—the last rite for the dying.)

Holy Communion is a sacrament that is most often celebrated within and as part of a service of worship. It is a communal meal; only in rare instances do persons partake of the elements of Holy Communion alone. When the Lord's Supper is celebrated as part of a service of worship, it is the highlight and the focus of the service. Some denominations celebrate this sacrament every Sunday. Others celebrate the sacrament once a month or once a quarter. Whatever the case, the celebration of Holy Communion is a high moment for all.

Did you catch the word *celebration* in that paragraph? Holy Communion is not a memorial meal for a dead martyr; it is a celebration of the presence of Christ with us.

The Sacrament of Holy Communion began when Jesus shared the bread and the cup with his apostles on the night he was betrayed and continued with the supper at Emmaus and the breakfast at Galilee. When Jesus gave his disciples the bread and cup, he said to do this in remembrance of him, and so we do.

In almost all churches, Jesus is felt to be very present in the act of Holy Communion. Most churches do not believe that the bread and juice actually become the body and blood of Jesus Christ, but most churches believe that Christ is a very real presence in the service of Holy Communion.

The Sacrament of Holy Communion consists of eating a bite of bread and drinking a sip of grape juice (many denominations do not use wine out of respect for children and for recovering alcoholics). The form of the bread varies widely. Some churches use a whole loaf of unsliced bread, others unleavened loaves such as pita bread, still others use disc-shaped wafers made from unleavened flour, and still others use very small squares of unleavened bread. In the same way, the container(s) for the juice to be used in the Communion can vary. Some use a single chalice or large (often stemmed) cup to hold the juice. Others use several chalices. Many churches use small individual cups of juice, often contained in a circular rack or tray. No one form of bread is the only right form; neither is any single container for the juice the only right way.

And just as the bread and the juice container vary, so may the style or form of distributing the bread and juice (called the elements) vary. In some churches, the elements are passed to persons as they sit in the pews. In other churches, folk come to the Communion rail that surrounds the chancel. There they take the elements or are given the elements by the liturgist, the pastor, or a server (who often serves them from behind the chancel or Communion rail). Worshipers at the chancel or Communion rail may partake of the elements standing or kneeling. In still other churches, worshipers come to the front of the church and there are given the elements of Holy Communion by the pastor, liturgist, or servers standing in front of the chancel or Communion rail.

As an usher, you must know how Communion is served in your church and the only way to learn that is to sit down with the pastor or the worship committee and go over it in great detail.

Yes, I hear you! You've been in this church for thirty years! You've participated in Holy Communion every time it has been offered. You know how it's done! But a word of advice: You know how it is carried out when you are a member of the congregation; but understanding how it is carried out when you are an usher, a part of the worship team, is very different. Please do not assume you know how it is done; go over it with the pastor or worship committee.

What are the basic functions of the team of ushers during the administration of the Sacrament of Holy Communion? In a simple sentence: Your job is to help persons participate in this sacrament as effortlessly and with as little confusion as possible. Only then will persons be able to focus on the sacrament and the presence of Christ and not get caught up in the mechanics of the process.

The first thing you must do is to follow to the letter the directions of the pastor or worship committee. Do not try to change these instructions, do not modify them, do not try shortcuts; simply *serve* without questioning. Following are several comments about some of the ways some congregations serve the Lord's Supper, but you must know how your congregation participates in this meal before attempting to serve as an usher at this high and holy moment.

Passing the Elements in the Pews

If the custom of your congregation is to pass the elements of Holy Communion to folk as they are seated in the pews, the team of ushers may be invited to the front of the sanctuary to receive the bread and the cup. In some situations, you will be served Holy Communion first; in other situations, you will be served after all others have been served. In either case, the pastor, celebrant (the person in charge of the Lord's Supper), or the liturgist will hand you either a plate containing the bread or the rack of single-service cups of juice to serve to the congregation (seldom is a single chalice passed in the pews). You will pass the plate of bread and the tray of juice cups in the pews much as you passed the offering plates during the taking of the offering. The bread is always passed first (because that is the sequence Jesus used in instituting this holy meal). In most situations of passing the elements in the pews, do not start the tray of cups until the entire pew has received the bread. This will avoid a "traffic jam" of one person trying to manage both the bread plate and the cup tray. The ushers will continue to pass the plate and the tray until all have received the bread and the juice; then the ushers will return the bread plates and the cup trays to the celebrant or pastor.

In some cases, the bread is passed first; and each person holds the piece of bread or wafer until the celebrant gives instructions. Then everyone eats the morsel of bread at the same time. Next, the tray of cups is passed; again everyone holds the cup until invited by the celebrant to drink of it as a congregation. Yes, this means that the ushers pass through the entire congregation twice, once with the bread, returning the bread plates to the chancel, then with the cup trays, returning them after all have received the cup.

Note that in some cases not everyone will choose to partake of the elements. In such a case, the person simply passes the bread plate or the cup tray to the person sitting next to her or him. No pressure should ever be placed on anyone to partake of the elements if a person chooses not to do so.

Note also that in almost all instances in which the bread and cups are passed in the pews, the members of the congregation place the empty cups in small, specially designed racks on the backs of the pews. In very rare situations, the empty cup trays are passed in the pews so that persons can return the cups.

People Coming Forward to Receive the Elements

The second way in which congregations regularly celebrate the Sacrament of the Lord's Supper is by the members of the congregation coming to the chancel rail, the Communion rail, or the front of the church to receive the elements. According to the tradition in the congregation, persons may receive the elements kneeling at the Communion or chancel rail; they may receive the elements standing at the chancel rail; or they may receive the elements from a server or servers standing at the chancel rail.

And the ways in which the members of the congregation receive the elements may vary also. In some congregations, a server holds out a tray of wafers or small cubes of unleavened bread, and each person takes a wafer or cube. Then the server holds out the tray or rack of individual Communion cups, and each person takes a cup. Whether kneeling or standing, all may eat of the bread at the same time and drink of the cup at the same time, or each person may eat the morsel of bread and drink the cup as it is received.

In still other situations, the sever places in the hand of each member of the congregation the morsel of bread and hands to each person the individual Communion cup. In still another form—and remember that all these forms, styles, and ways of celebrating Holy Communion are "right"—the server holds out a broken loaf of bread, and each person breaks off a piece of the bread. Or the server breaks a piece of bread from the broken loaf and hands it to the member of the congregation.

The offering of the cup may vary also. In place of the individual Communion cups, the server may hold one single chalice or large cup; each person either drinks from the cup or dips her or his morsel of bread into the cup before eating it. (This dipping of the bread into the cup is called *intinction*.) Occasionally where intinction is practiced, a person may eat the morsel of bread before the cup is passed to dip the bread into. In such a case, the server gives that person another piece of bread as that person receives the cup; this might even symbolize that Christ provides enough bread and more for all who hunger for his righteousness.

A further custom: In some settings, persons return to their pews as soon as they have received the elements. In other settings, they are welcome to remain in prayer at the Communion rail as long as they wish. And in still other settings, especially when persons receive the elements while kneeling, folk kneeling at the Communion rail who have received the elements remain kneeling in prayer until the liturgist or pastor has said a brief prayer for them. (These brief prayers are often called *table dismissals*.)

Now, what is the task of the usher during a service of Communion in which persons come to the front in order to receive the elements? Forgive a bit of flippancy, but the usher's tasks are three: *crowd control, traffic direction,* and our old friends *welcoming, comfort, and safety.*

Please understand thoroughly how Communion is handled in your church before you first serve as usher at a service of Communion. For example, in many churches, ushers stand at the back of the centermost aisle and, on direction from the liturgist, invite the folk sitting nearest the center aisle on both sides to stand and make their way down the center aisle to the Communion rail. In order to expedite movement, ushers standing at the Communion rail assist the members of the congregation in returning to their pews via the side aisles (rather than the center aisle). Ushers standing at the Communion rail are also there to assist persons in kneeling or in standing after they have knelt to receive the elements or to provide a hand for those who may be a bit unsteady on their feet as they stand to receive the elements.

If your church has more than a center aisle and two side aisles, customarily those sitting in the center pews come to the table first, then those seated in the side pews. Again, in most cases the ushers invite persons to the table commencing in the back of the sanctuary and working toward the front.

A couple of important things to remember as you invite persons to the chancel rail. First, this is not a time for conversation or small talk, nor is it a time to motion to someone and say, "OK," "You're next," or something of the sort. Simply say, "You are welcome at the Lord's Table."

Do not expect everyone to move toward the front of the church; some may choose to remain in their pews. Do not, ever, put any pressure on anyone to go to the Lord's Table if she or he chooses not to do so. On some occasions visitors may give you a questioning look or even ask you outright if they are allowed to partake of the Lord's Supper. If yours is a denomination that practices open Communion, that is, the Lord's Table is open to all, then again smile and say something like, "Yes, you (and your children) are most welcome at the Lord's Table."

And a third point, one that calls for careful diplomacy and love: If you notice a person sitting in a pew that you think would have difficulty walking to the front of the church to receive Communion (such as a person with a physical impairment or in some cases a very elderly person), ask that person in a quiet and kindly voice, "Would you like to be served here in your seat?" In many cases, the person will respond affirmatively. Then it is your task to report this to the Communion servers as discreetly as possible. The servers will take the bread and the cup to the persons you have identified and serve them as they remain in their pews.

When all have been served, either by passing the bread and cup in the pews or by coming forward to receive the elements, you as a team of ushers will return to your stations. You have completed your tasks of assisting in the Sacrament of the Lord's Supper.

7

WHEN THE SERVICE OF WORSHIP HAS ENDED

The service of worship—be it a service of Word and Table, that is, Holy Communion, or a service of Word alone, that is, including a sermon or the proclaimed Word of God—has ended. You have already taken the offering and returned to your station, or you have completed your responsibilities in the distribution of the elements of the Lord's Supper and have returned to your station. The liturgist or the pastor has just pronounced the benediction, and the organist or pianist has begun the postlude, the instrumental music played at the conclusion of a service of worship.

So what do you as an usher do now?
You're right! Your ministry is not quite over yet. You still have several tasks to perform. Let's list them here; you select the ones that are appropriate for you, given your station at one of the sanctuary doors or at the narthex door.

Watch carefully as people begin to gather their belongings and prepare to leave the sanctuary. Do any need help or assistance of any kind? Help with putting on coats? Assistance in gathering the items they brought into the sanctuary? This may be especially true of parents with small children; sometimes they simply do not have hands enough to carry Sunday school materials, Bibles, children's toys, coats, children's Sunday school craft projects, and the children themselves! Your ministry is to provide comfort, welcome, and safety. Offer gently to assist, but do not force yourself on anyone. You might offer to carry materials and objects rather than taking the hands of the children; some children may be reluctant to take the hand of a stranger or may feel uncomfortable doing so.

If yours is like many churches across our land, the pastor will be standing at the narthex door greeting worshipers as they leave the sanctuary. At least one usher (preferably two) should be stationed in the narthex at this time. You are here to assist in two ways:

One, you will help *members of the congregation* find coats, umbrellas, and other items left in the narthex. Offer to help persons with coats; do so with a genuine smile but with a minimum of words. Again, offer to hold objects for persons as they struggle with coats (especially heavy winter coats); offer to walk persons to their cars with church umbrellas if rain or snow is falling. (Your narthex does contain a couple of large golf-type umbrellas, doesn't it? Several of these are essential equipment for a narthex.) If the outside doors are closed due to inclement weather, open them for departing worshipers. Be especially aware of the needs of persons with mobility impairments; do all you can to make them comfortable and safe. This could run from extending a supporting arm for worshipers to holding doors open and clearing the way for persons on crutches or in wheelchairs.

The second form of assistance is for *the pastor* as she or he greets persons as they leave. Here's a hint. Stand to one side of the narthex (out of traffic flow, of course) facing the pastor and in such a position that he or she can see you. Give the pastor your full attention (but this does not mean trying to listen as she or he greets each member of the congregation). Instead, be ready at a moment's notice to run an errand for the pastor and the church member the pastor is greeting. Some examples of the "errands" a pastor might ask you to do? "Do we have any more cassette tapes of last week's service of worship? Mrs. Jones would like to take one to her father." "Mr. Smith here would like a copy of the current *Upper Room* magazine." "These folk are new in our community. Would you jot down their name, address, and telephone number for me so that I might visit them this week?" "The Johnsons here would like an additional copy of our pictorial directory. They are on the top shelf in the closet in the church office. Could you get one for them?" The list is endless—and sometimes surprising! Someone once said that this sounded like one of the usher's tasks is to be a "gofer" for the pastor as the pastor greets persons after the service. And that's exactly right! A request made by a church member as she or he is leaving a service of worship needs to be met immediately; the pastor should not have to ask a worshiper to step aside for a moment with the promise that she or he, the pastor, will get what the worshiper is requesting after everyone else has left.

All right. Everyone has left the sanctuary and the narthex. The pastor is collecting his or her things and is ready to return to the study. Are you finished yet?
Not quite.

The team of ushers might do a quick check of the entire sanctuary, picking up bulletins that have been left in the pews, straightening and aligning Bibles and hymnals in the pew racks, replacing pencils in the pew racks, and gathering the inevitable candy and gum wrappers that are left in the pews. Is it the ushers' task to check the thermostats, to turn off the lights, to turn off the sound system? If so, attend to it.

And the team might do a quick check of the narthex. Is all the equipment in the narthex back where it belongs? Has the pitcher of water been emptied and wiped out? Have the candlelighters been returned to their proper place? Have any supplies that were used during this service of worship been replaced? (Nothing is more frustrating than needing a facial tissue for a worshiper, only to discover that the box is empty.)

Then, when all of this has been completed, one item remains. You as ushers have been engaged in ministry this day. You have served the Lord by serving your congregation. You have given your best, striving to provide welcome, comfort, and safety for the worshiping congregation. Before you leave for a well-earned Sunday dinner, gather as a team of ushers for a prayer of thanksgiving, praising God for God's call on your life to serve in the ministry of ushering.

Depart to serve, with a song of praise on your lips.

8

THE MINISTRY OF USHERING AT SPECIAL TIMES

Church ushers may be called into ministry in times and situations other than the Sunday morning services of worship. Let's highlight a couple of these.

Ushers at Services of Revival

In some parts of our nation, special services of revival are held, often annually. These are times, usually other than Sunday morning, when the congregation gathers to be challenged, inspired, and reminded of all that God has done in and through Jesus Christ. A series of revival services of worship may last from a couple of evenings to an entire week. Very often, a special preacher is brought in to proclaim the Word; on some occasions a different person preaches each night. Sometimes, special musicians are invited to share their testimony in song. So what does the team of ushers do at a service of revival? Several things.

First, the ushers perform *all* those ministries that they perform at a regular service of worship. The emphasis is on welcoming and insuring comfort and safety.

Second, ushers should arrive well before the service of revival begins. This is especially true if outside musicians are arriving to take part in the service. The team of ushers should know in advance where the musicians will be when they share their testimony in music. Sometimes this may mean rearranging chairs in the choir loft or designating a portion of a front pew for the musicians. One usher should be assigned to the visiting musicians, insuring that the musicians have a place where they can warm up prior to the service of worship, that they know where the restrooms and drinking water are located, and that they understand where they are to offer their ministry during the revival service of worship and where they are to be seated during the other components of the service. Sometimes, musicians may need assistance with their equipment. A good usher will offer to assist in carrying equipment and will offer to help with the set up, but only if asked. An usher should never take it upon herself or himself to try to assemble the musicians' equipment without being invited to do so by the musicians.

Third, a component of many revival services of worship is an invitation on the part of the preacher to worshipers to come to the front of the sanctuary or to the Communion or chancel rail and to kneel or stand in prayer following the sermon. Ushers, again acting as unobtrusively as possible, should be ready to assist those who wish to come to the rail. Some may need a steadying arm; others may need assistance in arising from a kneeling position; sometimes worshipers at this time may need a facial tissue or a sip of water. Ushers are there to provide just such ministries.

Fourth, the team of ushers should remain for several moments after a service of revival has ended to tidy up the sanctuary. Since many revivals cover several consecutive nights (and since many smaller membership congregations are served by one-day-a-week volunteer custodians), a few moments spent straightening hymnals, picking up candy wrappers, and generally preparing the sanctuary for the next night's revival service of worship are moments very well spent.

Ushers at Weddings

The ushers from a church in which a wedding is to be held have a rather special set of ministries.

First, the ushering team from a congregation should recognize that the team will probably not be serving as ushers for the wedding. Traditionally, the bridal couple selects its own ushers.

Second, the ministry of ushering during the actual time of the wedding may be somewhat different from ushering at a regular service of worship. The pastor, the bridal couple, or, in some cases, the wedding planner, will be in charge of the wedding ushers.

These ushers will receive their specific instructions from one or more of these sources.

So what does the regular ushering team do? One or more of the ushering team should be present (but very unobtrusively so!) at the wedding rehearsal held in the church. The usher's task here is to help the wedding party be aware of and locate any items they might need for the wedding. Where are the restrooms and drinking fountains? Where can the bridal party leave things securely? Where are the lighting controls, the thermostat, the candlelighters, the couples' kneeler (if your church has and uses one. Want a fancy name? The kneeler is called a *prie-dieux*, meaning a place for two persons to pray together.). Also, help the wedding ushers locate such things as the facial tissues and cough drops, the wheelchair, the large umbrellas, and the other essential equipment in the narthex.

Additionally, one member of the regular ushering team might attend the wedding, arriving early enough to insure that doors are unlocked, lights are on, the thermostats are set correctly, and that all is in readiness. Again, as unobtrusively as possible, the usher should remain for the wedding service of worship to provide any assistance anyone in the extended wedding party may need.

Similarly, this usher might remain after the service is completed. In most situations, the wedding party is responsible for returning the facilities it has used to the state in which they were found. But sometimes this does not include the sanctuary itself. So, usher, do one of those quick checks of the sanctuary—hymnals in the racks, all facing the same direction? Bulletins and wrappers picked up and discarded? Any items left in the pews, in other words, "lost and found"? (For some reason, this is quite common at weddings!) Thermostats reset, lights off, doors locked, all in readiness for the next Sunday morning?

Good! You have carried out your ministry.

Ushers at Funerals

Slowly but surely, services of death and resurrection are returning from funeral chapels to churches, and this is exactly as it should be. Why should a person who has attended a church all her or his life have the final service of worship in any place but her or his church?

All the things that we said above about ushers at weddings goes for ushers at funerals with the following exceptions.

The pastor and the funeral director will be in charge. The family may choose ushers from among close friends, or the family may ask the pall bearers to serve as ushers. The regular ushering team is there to assist and to provide needed supplies and equipment.

As in other situations, point out to the funeral director and the funeral ushers the restrooms, drinking fountains, and other important locations in the church buildings. Provide information on where facial tissues, water, cough drops, and other supplies are located in the narthex. Ask the funeral director if she or he would like a box of facial tissue in the family pew.

Discuss with the funeral director where the family might wait before entering the sanctuary. In some cases, the family arrives last and the seating of the family marks the beginning of the service of death and resurrection. If this is the case, the family may choose to arrive at the church several minutes early and to wait in a convenient room before being seated in the sanctuary. If this is to be the case, select a room close to the sanctuary, preferably one with comfortable chairs. Equip it with facial tissues, a pitcher of water and paper cups, a waste receptacle, and so on. Be sure that the funeral director or the funeral ushers know the location of this room and the best way to move the family from there into the sanctuary.

In many cases, the regular team of ushers may wish to attend the funeral. Do so. Let each sit with her or his family; the regular team of ushers have no duties during the service of death and resurrection unless an emergency situation arises.

Again, linger after the service to straighten up the sanctuary for the next service of worship.

A Few Other Thoughts

Some churches are inviting couples and families to serve as ushers. Great! As we indicated earlier, youth and adults can fulfill all the ministries of ushering. Small children in the family can assist in handing out bulletins, but of course should not be counted on as door ushers, chancel ushers, or congregation ushers.

Once in a great while, perhaps once in a lifetime, a situation might arise when a member of the congregation is creating such a commotion that he or she needs to be removed. I recall worshiping in a large church when a young adult in the balcony started shouting in direct argument with the preacher's sermon. The whole congregation was instantly embroiled in this controversy. But two ushers very quickly and quietly moved to the young man's side and escorted him out. He continued to shout all the way out, his voice echoing down the stairs and out the front door. Unusual? Very much so. But ushers must be prepared for almost anything.

What about little children, you ask? What about when they begin to create a disturbance? Some of the older books on ushering devoted pages to how to direct the parents of such a child to take the child to an appropriate nursery. However, most preachers will tell you that they never notice a child crying during a sermon and are almost always unaware of any other disturbance that a youngster might be causing. Children belong in worship; it is not the usher's task to eject anyone from a service of worship, save for an outlandish disturbance such as described in the preceding paragraph. Realize that in today's culture most parents will voluntarily remove a child who is creating a major disturbance; the door usher can direct the parents to the most convenient area within the church to attend to the child's needs.

When—and If—the Unthinkable Happens

Remember one of the primary tasks of ushering is? Right—providing *safety* for those who are worshiping. If this has not already been accomplished in your church, you as an usher or team of ushers *must* do this: Contact your local fire department, ask one of their representatives to meet you in the sanctuary at an agreed upon time and work out together with that representative an *emergency evacuation plan* for your sanctuary. Please don't think this is something you can plan on the spur of the moment or that "everyone will know what to do." And don't give in to the temptation to work this out yourselves without the help of a specialist. With that specialist, go over exits, alternative exits, specific tasks of each of the ushers who are serving at the time, an external gathering place so that all can be counted, and all the other details that go into such a plan. Post this plan conspicuously and be sure every single usher knows her or his assignment in the event of such an emergency. Please do not neglect this; this is concerned not only with fire but with storm, tornado, hurricane, or any of those other terrible events that, God forbid, could take place. Preparedness is absolutely vital to saving lives! Another situation that we hope will never happen is an intrusion or robbery during a service. Each usher must be watchful and know where to go most efficiently to call for help from the police.

The Ministry of Ushering

More and more congregations are recognizing the importance of the ministry of ushering. While no usher has responded to the call to usher for self-glory or for praise and appreciation, many congregations do recognize their teams of ushers (and other members of the worship team) in various ways. If this is the case in your church, accept such recognition humbly and graciously. You have agreed to serve the Lord through this special ministry; let others express their thanks to you.

Your ministry is one of *welcoming* and *insuring comfort and safety* for all who come to worship God in your church. Serve the Lord with gladness and the Lord's people with graciousness.

Thanks for your unique ministry!

1. Throughout this booklet, we'll use some of the traditional terms for spaces within and around a church building. The *nave* is the area of the church in which worshipers sit. It's the space with the pews or chairs. The *chancel* is that raised area in the front (or the center, if you have a church in the round) where the Communion table is placed and where you'll usually find the pulpit and perhaps a lectern. In many churches, the chancel is surrounded in part by a chancel rail, and quite often folk kneel at the chancel rail to receive the Sacrament of our Lord's Supper. Sometimes, the entire area—nave and chancel—is called the *sanctuary*, although that word can have several other technical definitions.

2. The *narthex* is the area just outside the nave where you may find coatracks and umbrella stands, literature tables and bulletin boards. Some folk refer to this area as the vestibule or even the porch. It is the first part of the church the worshipers enter, and it is one of the "work stations" of the ushers.

3. *Paraments* are the colored cloths that cover the Communion table and the pulpit. Paraments are of different colors, each signifying a special Sunday or a season of the church year. A basic set includes purple, red, white, and green paraments. A liturgical or paraments calendar indicates which color is to be used on which Sundays. In most congregations, ushers are not responsible for changing the paraments, but ushers should know what color is to be used each Sunday and should include this quick visual check as part of their preservice duty.